EMPLOYEES R
WITH LOCK F
BATHROOMS
PLATFORM T
TANK

MARTYN THOMPSON
WORKING SPACE

foreword by Emma Balfour
designed by Andrew Egan – CoolGraySeven

hardie grant books
MELBOURNE · LONDON

CONTENTS

FOREWORD

I have known Martyn Thompson for 25 years. We worked together often when I first started modeling. I liked him from the start; he had a quiet willfulness that I responded well to. I also have the dubious pleasure of being the only model he's reduced to tears (pure frustration on both our parts… that and the '80s side ponytail). We've stayed in touch ever since.

Martyn has always done his own thing and isn't afraid to push his own boundaries to explore what he finds engaging. He has maintained and built upon his unique aesthetic and working method, never limiting himself.

In this book he has chosen to photograph the spaces that people work in. These environments have mostly unintentionally become an extension of people's work and creativity. Rooms show the marks of process and passion, spaces shaped by function, necessity and chaos. Very few of the chosen spaces in this book have been designed as such. They have evolved and grown.

It is the unconscious exposure of their inhabitant's inner world that Martyn captures beautifully in this series of pictures. He has concentrated on the mood and feel of the spaces and highlighted the details he likes.

He has chosen the good bits to show us, the bits that sing and make us in turn feel happy and inspired.

Emma Balfour

Sydney, May 2013

DINOSAUR DESIGNS
Designers

In 1983, I co-opened a shop called Ox
in Sydney's Taylor Square selling the
clothes I made in my kitchen. One day,
an art student came in and asked my
roommate Linda, who often worked the
store for me, if he could sell his
jewelry there. Linda thought it a good
fit and I agreed. That art student turned
out to be Stephen Ormandy, which I
didn't know until he told me the story
years later.

Louise Olsen and Stephen Ormandy started
Dinosaur Designs with Liane Rossler in
Sydney in the late '80s. Their chunky,
colorful resin jewelry was an immediate
hit. Over the years, they've continued
to evolve this unique product, a rare
feat in fickle Sydney. Homewares soon
followed, and precious metals have
now been added to the mix; each piece
individually crafted in their rather
groovy factory by a gang of young
Sydneyites. There is a great spirit
of community here.

HELENE NGUYEN-BAN
Art Collector

After I'd finished putting together my
last book, *Interiors*, there was quite a
bit of material left over - and most of
it was of artist's studios. But I wanted
my next book to be about more than just
that. A friend suggested I broaden the
idea to "workspaces," an idea that
took flight. As the project advanced, it
morphed into something broader, yet the
essence of each space reflected something
that is always present in an artist's
studio: passion for what you do. The
owner of this Parisian apartment,
Helene Nguyen-Ban, is a passionate art
collector. The interior architecture,
carefully understated by Elliot Barnes,
brings her collection to life. Art is
the central presence in this space.
Every piece is notable.

CLEVELAND'S
Salon & Café

My annual trip to Sydney starts
immediately after Christmas when
everything in that city seems to be
closed. Arriving much in need of a
haircut, I wandered through Surry
Hills eventually stumbling across
"Cleveland's," a salon/café. It's a two
man show – Harry Levy makes the coffee
and Patrick Casey is the hair guy. Mid-
cut, I realized it would make a good
story. In New York I am so surrounded by
big corporate excess; there is something
very refreshing and contemporary about
the dual-use of this small space.

Ladies

· WASH, CUT & BLOWDRY $85

COLOUR BY CONSULTATION

Gents

· WASH, CUT & FINISH $70
· CUT THROAT $20

Sa

· PAGE
· PIN CU
· VICTOR
· BOUFF

· THE EA
· CREW
· FADE
· POMPA
· GH

Open

7 DAYS=

OUTDOOR
NATURAL
STRENGTH
& FITNESS
CLASSES
YOUR BEST BODY IN 2013

SURRY HILLS
STARTING JAN 21

FILLING FAST
6 weeks intro special $299

0401 084 238
www.surryhillsfitness.com

HUNGRY
MONDAYS

PICK UP SPOT $9

www.facebook.com/hungrymondays

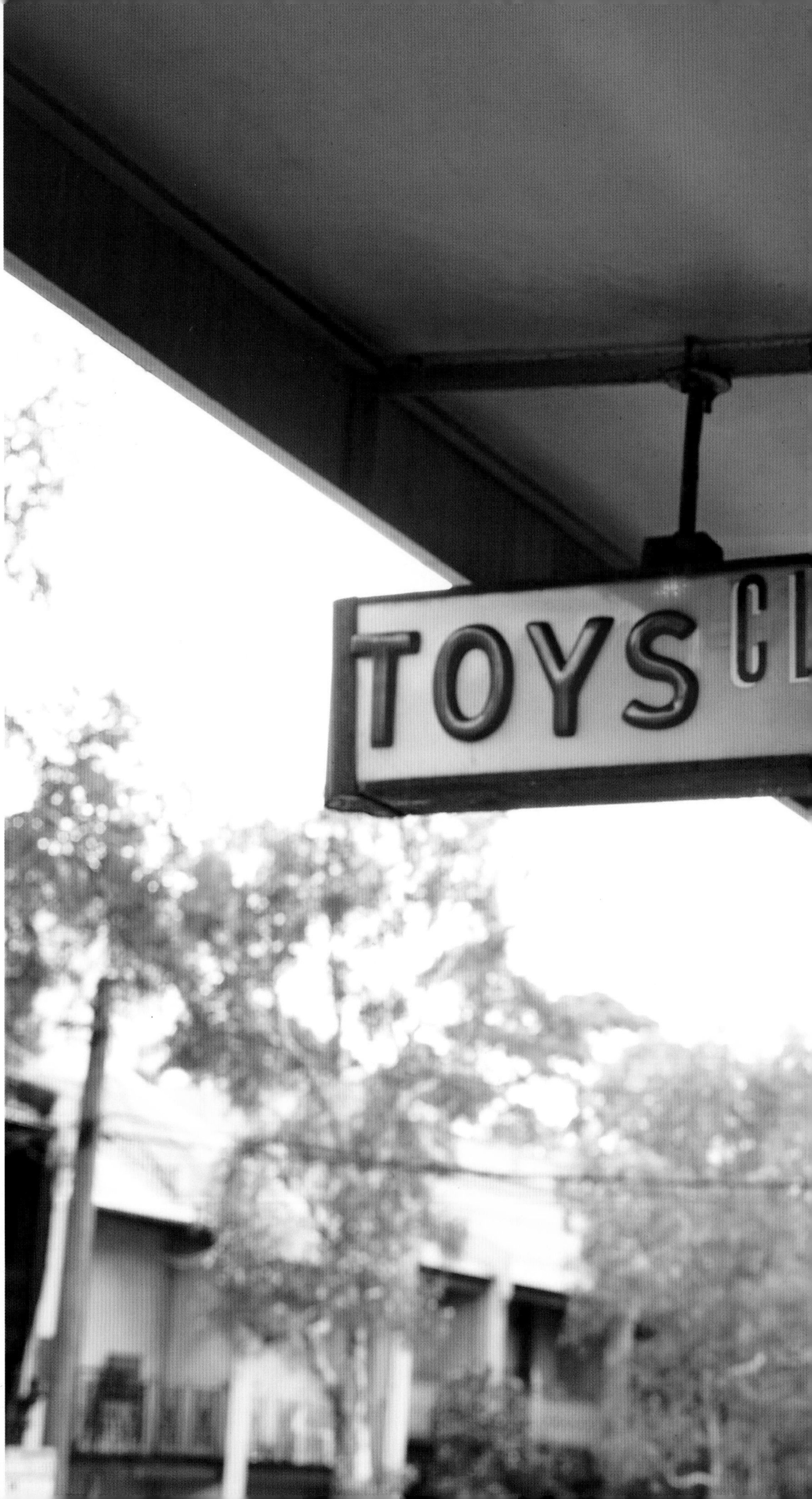
TOYS

PHYLLIS & IZZY
JEWELERS

The first summer I spent in Provincetown,
the old Portuguese fishing town turned
bohemian retreat on Cape Cod, I heard
whispers of the legendary locals,
Phyllis and Izzy. I met many people
wearing their jewelry, all of whom
seemed thrilled to have actually
gained access to their house and shop
- a local landmark.

The couple heralded from New York's
Greenwich Village where jeweler Phyllis
had met and married Israel "Izzy" Sklar,
an artist and musician turned talented
jeweler under Phyllis' tutelage. They
had been in Provincetown since 1961.
I eventually fell into favor and was
allowed to take some pictures one
autumnal afternoon. Over the years,
Izzy's obsessive collecting had combined
with their many mementos, paintings and
drawings into a marvelous mess; a jam-
packed personal history.

When I showed them the photos I'd taken,
they gave me the drawing on page 48: "We
Have Proof!" Sadly, they are both gone
now. Phyllis passed away in 2010 and
Izzy followed in 2012.

TELL ME
THE TRUTH
ABOUT
LOVE

TEN POEMS BY

W. H. AUDEN

BRAD GREENWOOD
Painter

In 2011, I co-curated a series of POP
UP art happenings with my friend and
silkscreening teacher, Charles Lahti.
Brad Greenwood was a regular contributor
to these events, which we hosted
under the banner of "THE TREE." He had
recently returned to painting full-time
after working for many years in the
event and funding side of the art world
at MoMA PS1.

To promote the shows, I shot mini-
stories of the artists at work for our
social media sites. The story I shot
for Brad is seen here. Ultimately, this
series of paintings became his first big
solo show. I love all of his references
lying around and the easy connection
between the imagery and the art.

MARGARET NOLAN
Graphic Designer

When I'm working on a project I always
seek intermittent advice from my friend,
Penny Galwey. I thought I'd nearly
finished this one when Penny said, "There
aren't any real offices in the book" – a
valid point.

I don't often have a reason to go to
"real" offices, so I tried to think of
people who might lead me to some spaces
that would fit the bill. I was in Sydney
at the time, my last destination for
this project. Margaret Nolan came to
mind. The home she shares with her
husband, Ronan Sulich, has always had
a sophistication beyond most, but I'd
never seen the offices of her graphic
design company, The Collective.

The space is very simple and it's all
about the art. The only thing you notice
are the paintings. I think that's a
really lovely way for an office space
to work.

THIERRY DREYFUS
Lighting Designer

Tucked into a quiet corner off the
busy Rue Etienne Marcel, this office,
the base of Parisian Thierry Dreyfus,
is a luminous junkyard of ideas and
industry. The intense Dreyfus creates
light installations for many fashion
shows - his clients include Yves Saint
Laurent, Ann Demeulemeester, Calvin
Klein, and Raf Simons. He designed
the remarkable Rupture light system
for Flos and also takes a beautiful
photograph. It's a tiny space jam-
packed with past projects, lights
he's working on, objects he's found
and many packets of cigarettes. Plans
are often sketched directly on a wall.
There is a complete disregard for
anything remotely domestic.

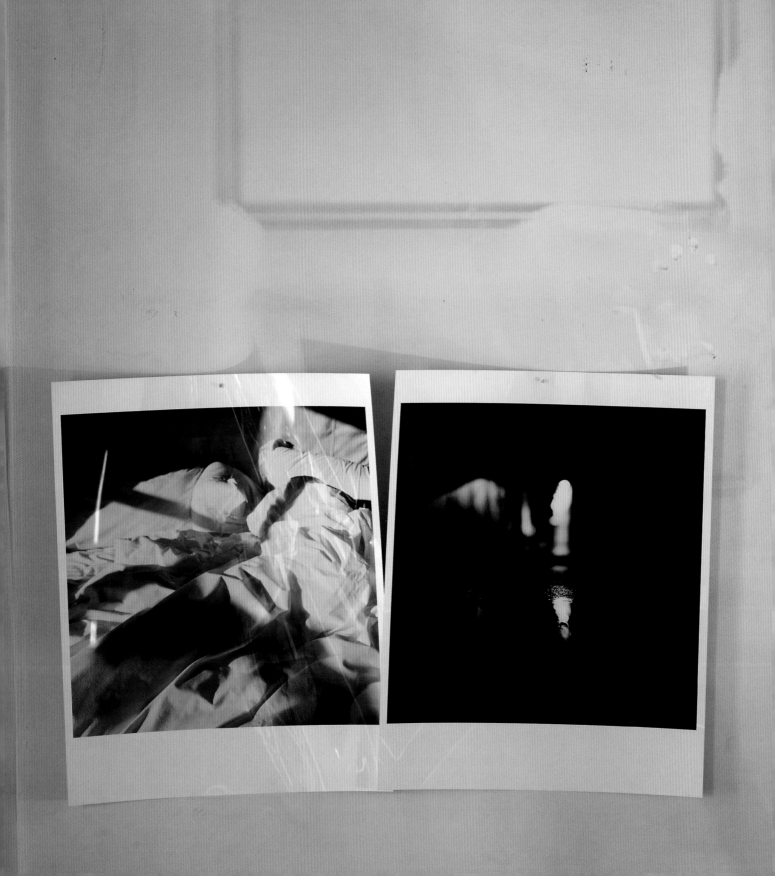

CAPUCINE GEAGEA
Editor

We only had an hour or two to capture
this room as it was the last stop on my
Paris trip before heading off to Berlin,
but it was an absolute "must have."

The home of Capucine Geagea – who
started her webzine *Plume Voyage* in this
sitting room – is the ultimate chic at-
home office. Overlooking the Louvre, it
exhibits the often daunting stylization
that overwhelmed me when I lived in
Paris in the 80s; that particularly
refined French mix of the ancient and the
contemporary – not the sort of place you
came across while growing up in Sydney.

7/15

E.R.BUTLER
Manufacturer

I really wanted to photograph a factory
and I found the perfect place in E.R.
Butler & Co., the custom hardware
manufacturing business of Rhett
Butler. Rhett combines his knowledge
of historical process with modern
technology to create his exquisitely
crafted pieces, an experimental mindset
that has led him into collaborations
with artists such as Ted Meuhling and
Hella Jongerius.

Although it was under renovation when
I visited, I still found a real charm
in this very raw space out in Red
Hook, Brooklyn. It's a huge place;
they're even building a pool for
swimming in the summer. I love the
super blokey feel with the pin-up
girls stuck on the fridge - kind of
like an archetypical garage - and
yet they produce such rarefied things.
Note the birdcage sitting on the chest
marked "inflammable." It's not your
typical factory.

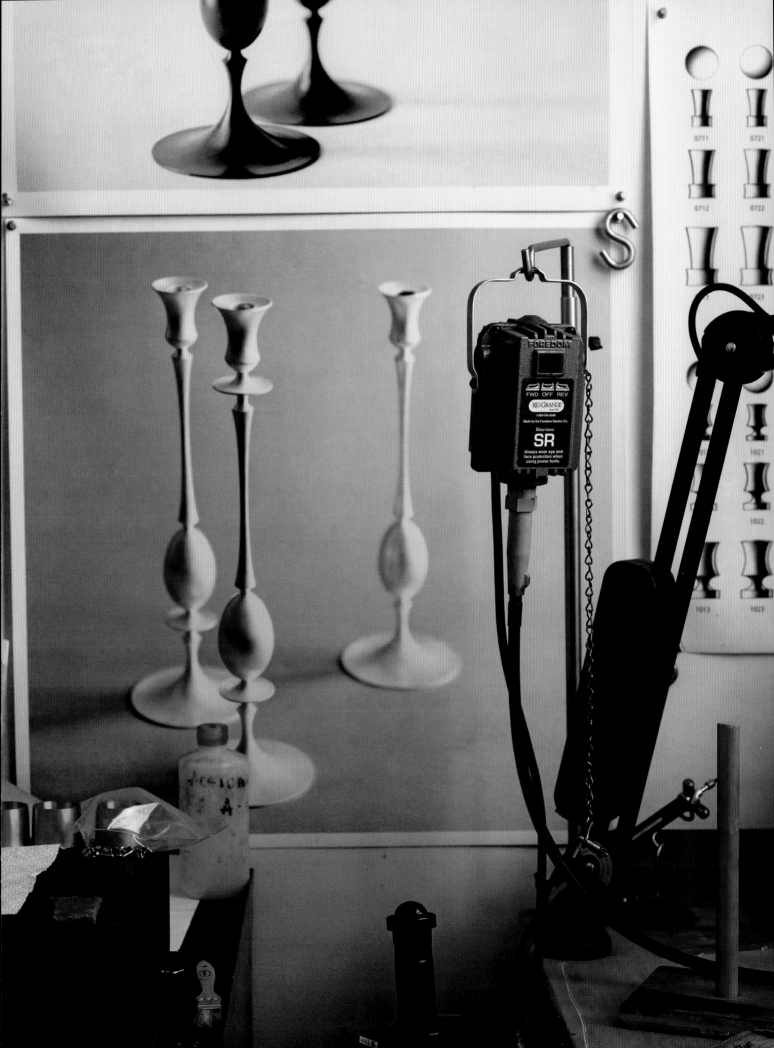

THE GAABS
Creative consultancy

I'd come to Berlin in pursuit of two
things; people to feature for this book
and the person I now refer to as my
boyfriend. Generally, the first of these
things happened by day and the second
by night, which meant I was pretty
tired most of the time I was there (and
consequently kept getting lost on the
transit system).

I arrived at THE GAABS much in need of
a cup of tea. Despite the fact that
things were pretty busy, they managed
to conjure one up for me. Marcus, a
photographer, and Christiane, an art
director, run their creative consultancy
THE GAABS from this lofty space in
Kreuzberg, the same space where they
publish *I Love You* magazine. This
workspace has no sophisticated build-
out, yet it's effective. There is a
clear sense of functionality, but it
remains luxuriously raw.

A MISTAKE IS
NOT ALLWAYS
WRONG

ANNABEL ADIE
Ceramicist

Generally, the work I do is ultra "pre-planned." However, in delightful (and at times terrifying) contrast, nearly all of this book was shot on the fly. We arrived in Paris with only a hotel reservation and the phone number of Marie Le Fort, a journalist friend-of-a-friend and complete godsend whose every direction turned out a gem.

Our first stop was to visit Annabelle Adie, a designer and ceramicist whose studio is in the home she shares with her husband in Montmartre. Hers is one of those Parisian apartments where each room leads to another, ultimately guiding you in a full circle. The distinct color palette and quirkiness of her aesthetic is present throughout the apartment, making it difficult at times to discern the living spaces from the work spaces. There is something very freeform and organic about her work – a feeling of being in motion. Some of it looks as though things have gone wrong, like the candlestick on the table that is crooked. We are not looking at perfection, we are looking at accidental mistakes and how beautiful they are.

Make sure you keep your GardenGnomes checked

CINDY SHERMAN
Artist

Generally if *W* magazine calls, I'm
always excited to see what they want.
When they said "Cindy Sherman" my
heart skipped a beat, but then they
said "cupboards" and I wasn't so sure.
However, I couldn't resist a chance to
meet the iconic photographer.

I expected an imposing giant, a virtual
landmark, and was shocked by the
agelessly beautiful Sherman, so polite
and unassuming, who granted us free
reign to rummage through her things –
which we did. Her studio is a treasure
trove of couture and costuming, wigs,
prosthetics, cosmetics, shoes, etcetera.

The pictures accompanied an article
about Sherman on the eve of her big
retrospective at the MoMA.

JEREMY WADE
Choreographer

I hadn't been to Berlin since the late
'70s when, as a teenager and under the
spell of David Bowie and the mythical
Isherwood "cabaret" Berlin of the 1930s,
I made the necessary pilgrimage to this
legendary outpost. It's changed a lot
since then. Jeremy Wade, an American
dancer and choreographer, is part of
the new generation of artists who has
made Berlin home. It's a city accustomed
to foreigners with a thriving, well-
supported arts community.

Intense and frenetic on stage, I'd seen
Jeremy perform many times in New York
and was surprised by the organic calm
of his base in Neukölln. I love the
subtle play of green and orange.
There's nothing opulent here and yet
it feels very rich to me - a kind of
simple sophistication.

FRANCESCA RAFT
Painter

I've known Francesca most of my working
life. Our bond was cemented years ago
as we were two Australian ex-pats, one
model and one fashion photographer,
cast adrift on the Parisian fashion
scene – both a little lonely as we'd
bravely moved there not really knowing
a soul. Today she lives in Sydney and
is a painter with a studio in the attic
of her house. She paints very somber
landscapes. Even when she was very
young, I always felt there was something
very "old soul" about her; her paintings
reflect that.

GOLCONDE

Ashram

This little-known modernist gem,
designed by Antonin Raymond and George
Nakashima in 1935, forms part of
the Sri Aurobindo Ashram. Located in
Pondicherry, India, the calm inside
these walls is in complete contrast to
what's often happening on the outside.

These pictures were taken some years
ago for French *Vogue*, years before I
understood that meditation is work
in and of itself. I love that this
building is so stark yet simultaneously
so tactile. The result is one of
absolute focus.

HAZZY BEE
Street Artist

A.k.a. Harry Levy, Hazzy Bee is a street
artist I met at Cleveland's where he
puts to work his other passion, making
coffee. He took me on a quick tour of
the Sydney suburb of Newtown where the
local council has commissioned a lot
of his street art. Harry explained
that this makes it legal. In its
uncommissioned form, the same work is
classified as "graffiti" and is illegal.

On a side note, I spend a lot of time in
Chicago where the threat of "graffiti" has
caused a complete ban on spray paint. You
can't buy it anywhere within city limits
– but that's not stopping anyone.

HazzyBee ❤

··· ŲMNY
Ţ4Ţ···

HILL END PRESS
Print Makers

"Hill End?" Just a few hours drive from Sydney, I was told. Six and a half hours as it turns out, but then, Australia is a big place (and navigation was never my strong suit).

This 18th-century gold-rush town beyond the Blue Mountains of New South Wales, with its charming corrugated-iron shanties and fields of kangaroos, has been an artists' colony on and off since the 60s. Bill Moseley and Genevieve Carroll, residents for the last eight years, are working hard to keep the past alive – not only by maintaining these historic buildings, but also through employing various antiquarian processes in their art. Printmaking at the Hill End Press is heroically carried out on turn-of-the-century machines the couple picked up for next to nothing; most people nowadays opt for the convenience of an inkjet printer at home.

PATRICK MARBER
Playwright

Fiona Golfar introduced playwright
Patrick Marber to me, describing how he
worked in a "trailer in the middle of
a field," quite fulfilling the romantic
image I have of that profession – the
lonely writer, solitary and isolated,
slaving away in the middle of nowhere.

However, this trailer is only a skip
away from his house, and Patrick, a
family man, is likely to be found
playing cricket with his children
in the garden. As someone who has
an extremely messy desk, I'd been
intrigued when prior to my visit Patrick
informed me that his lair was devoid
of paraphernalia. But he spoke the
truth. The trailer functions as a sort
of sanctuary; a place to think, drink
coffee and make a few notes.

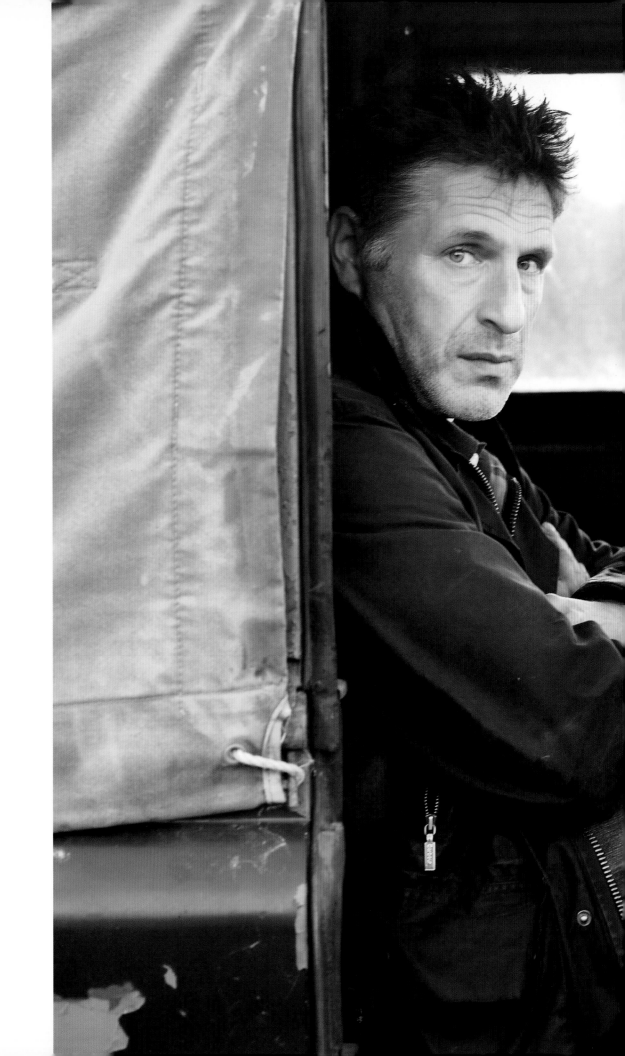

The Spectrum
Performance Space

New York has plenty of expensive shows
on Broadway, but there's an abundance of
alternative and affordable performance
going on off-, off-, and even further
off-Broadway. It's one thing to really
love about the city. There are layers
of creation happening everywhere, even
potentially in your living room, which
is quite literally the case here.

Performance artists Nick Gorham and Gage
of the Boone were looking for somewhere
to live when they stumbled across this
moody mirrored space behind a bar in
Bushwick. They moved in and transformed
it into a universally accessible space,
now a central hub for queer art and
performance in New York City.

JOHN MELFI
Executive Producer

So many places hold an almost
mythological quality in my imagination
- the result of films seen and books
read. Driving down from New York, I was
excited to finally get to see Baltimore,
home of Divine and the amazing movies of
John Waters that I'd seen at Sydney's
now long lost Paris Theatre – the one
that played those "weird" movies when
I was a teenager.

But we never got quite there. This film
set, 40,000 square feet of industrial
space for the Netflix show *House of
Cards*, was actually situated somewhere
just outside of Baltimore, right off
the highway between a KFC and a Dunkin'
Donuts. Though a typical workspace for
someone who works in television or
film, I found it to be a very surreal
environment; you're constantly passing
through what appear to be different
realities. One minute you are on set
in a very believable middle-class
sitting room, and the next you're being
golfcarted through a cavernous warehouse
for lunch at fold-up tables with plastic
knives and forks.

John Melfi's job? As Executive Producer,
he not only has to find a way to make the
economics of the show's budget work, but
he has to convince all sorts of stars
and talents to spend a year there, not
to mention keep them *all* happy – not
so easy.

NATHALIE LETE
Designer

It's amazing how quickly I've become
dependent on my iPhone as a navigation
device. Once upon a time, I'd go to work
with a map and a set of directions,
but now I just assume I'll find it on
the phone, totally forgetting about the
possibility of hitting a no-service
zone. Naturally, this was exactly what
occurred when I went to the outskirts
of Paris in search of Nathalie Lete;
somehow, we still found each other.

Lete's studio is a miasma of Lete
product – all feminine and childlike
but with a rather macabre twist. She's
a very busy woman with a remarkable
level and scope of productivity. There
were things absolutely everywhere,
all designed and produced by her. Her
drawings are transformed into ceramics,
textiles, toys, rugs and jewelry. It's
fascinating to see the many stages of
her creativity.

HARLAND MILLER
Painter

Harland Miller loves a cup of tea and
like many English folk, has a particular
way of making it. Typically, this is
based in some ancient family folklore
and involves turning the pot a number of
times in a certain direction or having
the water at a very specific temperature
as it is poured from the kettle.

I first heard of Harland a number of
years ago when he wrote a book titled
Slow Down Arthur, Stick to Thirty, about
a David Bowie fanatic. I read it on the
enthusiastic recommendation of a mutual
friend of ours and loved it. All three
of us, it turns out, have shared an
enthusiasm for Bowie since puberty.

The studio we see here is on a remote
industrial estate in Yorkshire near the
town of Bridlington where Harland grew
up. He rented it for the summer to make
these paintings as he needed a large
space for the poured paint to dry flat.
They would be the last in the Penguin
Book cover series that he is famous for.

Our mutual friend had told me that
Harland was working from a WW2 aircraft
hangar. Rather exotic, I thought. But in
true Chinese whispers style, the hangar
turned out to be next door.

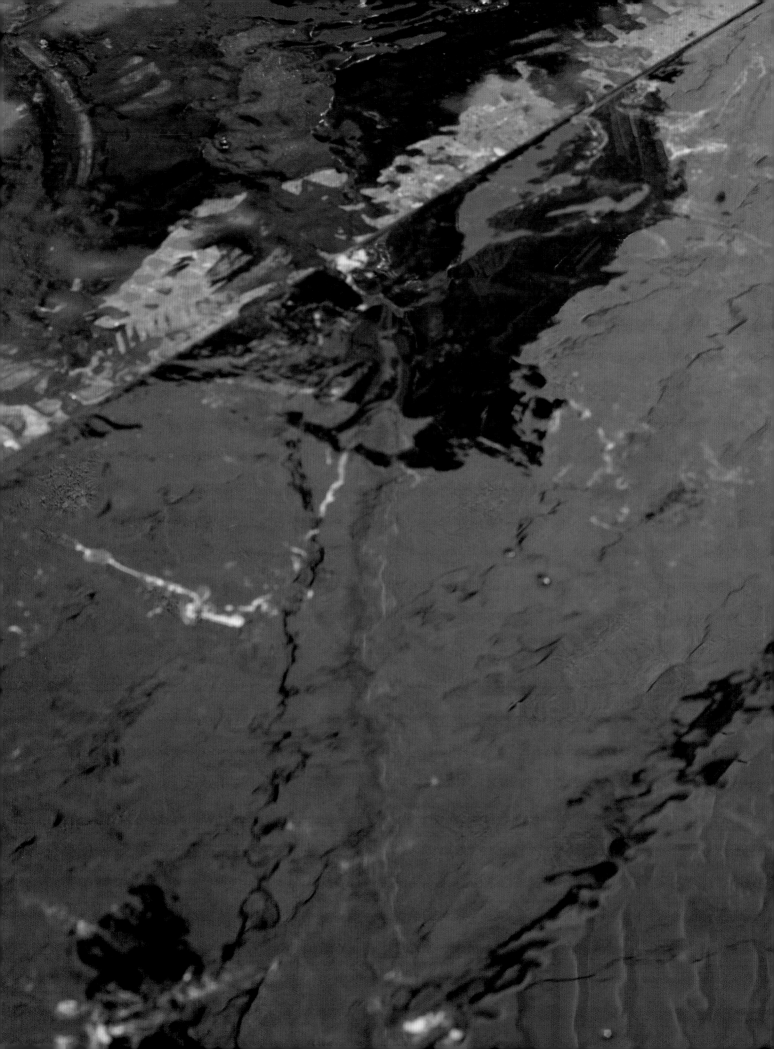

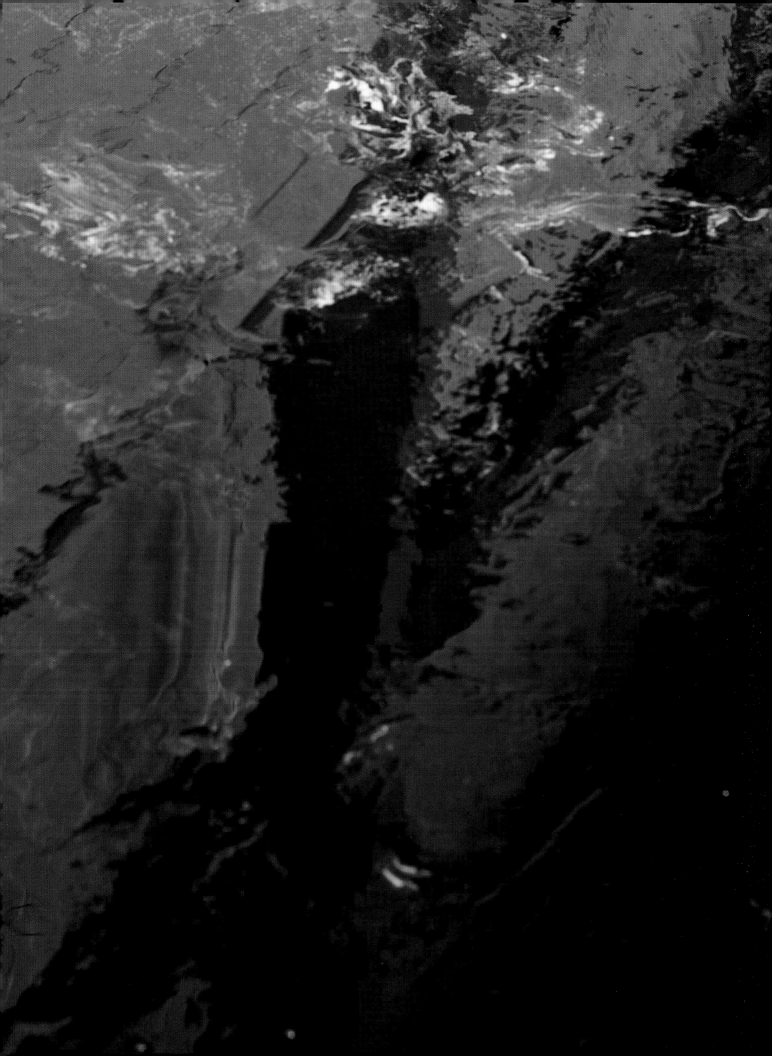

MEADHAM KIRCHHOFF
Fashion Designers

There is nothing I don't like about
this space. The last stop on a five-day
trip to London (that had been something
of an organizational juggling act),
I had only a few hours at Meadham
Kirchhoff's studio before heading back
to the airport. Despite the mayhem,
my heart stopped racing as soon as I
got there. The space had all of the
ingredients I love to photograph; a
sort of contemporary bohemian madness
and quirky visual energy that makes for
great pictures. My friend Nikki Tibbles,
the great florist and dog rescuer, had
made the introduction. Meadham Kirchhoff
is the fashion design team of Edward
Meadham and Ben Kirchhoff. They met as
students at Central Saint Martins and
have been producing a collection since
2010. Their clothes are as inspired and
eclectic as the space suggests.

Shoes + heels yellow gold beads 1 pair

Shoes + heels blue / blue beads 1 pair

Shoes + he

EMMA BALFOUR
Poet

Emma was always the most unlikely
model and rarely wanted to play by the
rules. The down-to-earth tomboy who was
most comfortable in jeans and a baggy
sweater, Emma didn't care to look the
part and remained generally unruffled by
the chaos of "glamour" surrounding her.
I was always a bit intimidated by her;
she seemed to bypass the superficial.

Her home in Sydney is a simple reflection
of young family life – a collection of
kids' drawings, some naïve paintings by
Chaz Glover and intimate photographs
by her husband, Andrew Cowen. Her great
escape is horseback riding, but given
a quiet moment Emma retreats to her bed
to work on her poetry; she is currently
putting together a second collection.

Xmas 2010

MARTYN THOMPSON

Not one to be caught lounging around, Thompson's photographic career was set in motion some 30 years ago when he began shooting the "Made in My Kitchen" fashion he was producing at the time. As it turned out, his images attracted more attention than the clothes themselves, launching a career that continues to make a profound visual impact today.

An expat of Sydney, Australia, Thompson was seduced at an early age first by glam rock and later the dynamic youth movements exploding in the early 80s. He was particularly captivated by the aesthetic of Vivienne Westwood and Malcolm McLaren's subversive early collections, and the music of artists such as Siouxsie and the Banshees.

Later in the decade, after several years in Paris, Thompson relocated to London where he began to move from fashion photography into the world of interiors. Perhaps due to his intellectual curiosity and a love of the lived environment, he began to develop a new, atypical approach to documenting interiors and architecture. In a Martyn Thompson image the human and the environment are always connected - the ordinary can become something enigmatic. His mastery of natural light is a skill that has made him highly sought after for still-life and product photography.

A keen advocate of change and experiment, his work today has evolved to include video, mixed-media print work and 3D installation, often reflecting an artisanal aesthetic borne out of his love of craft.

Thompson has contributed editorial to some of the world's most respected global publications including *Architectural Digest*, *W*, *The New York Times* and *Vogue*. Commercially, he has created acclaimed imagery for many of the world's leading brands including Tiffany & Co., Ralph Lauren, Hermès and MAC cosmetics. In addition to working on a number of published titles, including two books with regular collaborator Ilse Crawford, Thompson released *Interiors* (Hardie Grant Books), which overflows with iconoclasts and the beautiful spaces they inhabit.

THANK YOU

I've had a lot of help putting this book together.

Thanks to Andrew Egan and his team at CoolGraySeven for the effortless and elegant design, and to journalist Mallery Roberts Morgan for organizing some thoughts into facts and kick-starting the writing process.

I'd be lost without my chief technician and working partner in crime, Evan Strang, and the delightful daily drama of Skyler Smith.

Thank you to all who helped me find the people that I photographed – Marie Le Fort, Fiona Golfar, Ismael Goldsztejn-Seck, Samuel Hodge, Aaron Peasley and Nikki Tibbles.

For her beautiful words – Emma Balfour.

And for their advice and patient consultation – Penny Galwey, Dove Drury Hornbuckle, Louise Olsen, Karen McCartney and Paul McNally.

Finally, all the subjects of this text – some of you I've known for years and others I met only fleetingly – a big thank you to everyone who let me infiltrate and illustrate their inspiring working worlds.

—

Published in 2013 by Hardie Grant Books

Hardie Grant Books (Australia)
Ground Floor, Building 1
658 Church Street
Richmond, Victoria 3121
www.hardiegrant.com.au

Hardie Grant Books (UK)
Dudley House, North Suite
34–35 Southampton Street
London WC2E 7HF
www.hardiegrant.co.uk

Cataloguing-in-Publication is available from www.nla.gov.au
ISBN 9781742706122

Publishing Director: Paul McNally
Concept and Photography: Martyn Thompson
Design and Art Direction: CoolGraySeven
Writers: Martyn Thompson and Mallery Roberts Morgan
Copy Editor: Ashley Mikal
Production: Todd Rechner

Colour reproduction by Splitting Image Colour Studio
Printed and bound in China by 1010 Printing International Limited